Silk Screening

CHERRY LAKE PUBLISHING • ANN ARBOR, MICHIGAN

by Lyz Luidens and Camille Griffin

CHERRY LAKE Publishing

A Note to Adults: Please review the instructions for the activities in this book before allowing children to do them. Be sure to help them with any activities you do not think they can safely complete on their own.

A Note to Kids: Be sure to ask an adult for help with these activities when you need it. Always put your safety first!

Published in the United States of America by Cherry Lake Publishing
Ann Arbor, Michigan
www.cherrylakepublishing.com

Series Editor: Kristin Fontichiaro
Photo Credits: Cover and page 1, Alan Levine / tinyurl.com/lo7trag /
CC-BY-SA-2.0; pages 4, 5, 7, 9, 13, 14, 18, 21, 22, 23, 25, 27, and 29,
Lyz Luidens; page 11, Chicago Art Department/tinyurl.com/oapvrdc/
CC-BY-2.0; pages 17 and 19, Rebekah Modrak; page 20, Memphis CVB/
tinyurl.com/l6lda52/CC-BY-ND-2.0

Library of Congress Cataloging-in-Publication Data
Luidens, Lyz.
Silk screening/by Lyz Luidens and Camille Griffin.
    pages cm.—(21st century skills innovation library.)
Audience: Grade 4 to 6.
Includes bibliographical references and index.
ISBN 978-1-63362-379-8 (lib. bdg.)—ISBN 978-1-63362-435-1 (pdf) —
ISBN 978-1-63362-407-8 (pbk.)—ISBN 978-1-63362-463-4 (ebook)
1. Screen process printing—Juvenile literature. I. Griffin, Camille
(Juvenile literature author) II. Title.
TT273.L78 2016
686.2'316—dc23   2015011198

Cherry Lake Publishing would like to acknowledge the work of The Partnership for
21st Century Skills. Please visit *www.p21.org* for more information.

Printed in the United States of America
Corporate Graphics.
July 2015

21st Century Skills INNOVATION LIBRARY

Contents

Chapter 1   **What Is Silk Screening?**   4

Chapter 2   **Creating Your Image**   11

Chapter 3   **Final Preparations**   21

Chapter 4   **Time to Print!**   25

Glossary   30
Find Out More   31
Index   32
About the Authors   32

Chapter 1

What Is Silk Screening?

Have you ever wondered how images are transferred onto posters, T-shirts, and other items? One common way of reproducing images is known as screen printing, or silk screening. Screen printing is the process of pushing ink through a mesh screen onto the material you want to print on.

Screen printing is a fun way to customize your own shirts, posters, and other items.

With a little practice, you will be able to screen print like a pro.

People all around the world have been screen printing for hundreds of years. Originally, the process was used mainly for the creation of religious artwork. Much later, it became a popular technique for creating everything from advertisements to decorative artwork. Today, it is considered one of the most accessible forms of **printmaking**. Everyone from beginners

Screen Printing Success

One group of people who have found screen printing success are the students behind Detroit Community High (DCH) Apparel. Producing posters, T-shirts, tote bags, and almost anything else you can imagine, DCH Apparel began operating in fall 2012. The program was originally started at the high school to give students a voice in their school dress code. Since then, it has won awards and received national news coverage. Today, DCH Apparel has grown into a school-based business run by DCH students. It offers design and printing services to anyone who needs them.

One of the students who helps run DCH Apparel says that screen printing is one of the most productive things she does. When she first began, she thought that it would be a very difficult and complicated process to learn. After a little practice, she now says that it's actually a lot of fun and that the more you do it, the easier it gets!

to experienced **makers** can do it. As long as you have the proper tools, you can create a professional-quality screen print!

Screen printing tools and materials can be found at most art supply stores. They don't take up much space, they aren't very expensive, and they are easy to store. You also don't need a lot of space for the actual screen printing process. As a result, it is easy to get started with screen printing.

The first tool you will need is a framed printing screen. Screen printing frames and screens look a lot like a window screen. Originally, the mesh screens stretched across screen printing frames were made of silk, which is why you may sometimes hear screen printing referred to as "silk screening." Today, the mesh on screen printing frames is almost always made from a material called nylon.

The frame is usually made of wood or metal. The mesh screen is pulled tight across the frame and held in place with heavy-duty staples. Metal frames are usually made of aluminum, which is very light, and they never **warp**. Wooden frames tend to be heavier

On the left is a screen ready for printing. On the right is an unprepared mesh screen.

and can warp over time. Warping is especially likely with lighter woods. You can't print with a warped screen. However, most store-bought frames can be trusted to last quite a while.

You have the option to buy a frame and mesh separately, and then stretch the mesh across the frame yourself. You can also build your own frame if you know how and have the right tools. Starting off with a store-bought frame takes less time and works just fine for most projects.

Your screen must be larger than the design you plan on printing by at least a few inches on each side. Producing clean, crisp prints is much easier to manage with a screen that leaves the design plenty of breathing room.

Equally as important to screen printing as a screen and frame is the ink. You can buy screen printing ink at most art supply stores. It comes in a few different varieties. There is screen printing ink for fabric, for paper, and for metal and plastic. It is very important to choose the proper ink for the surface you'll be printing on. Otherwise, it may not dry well or last as long as it should. You should also be careful to buy ink that is

A squeegee is one of a screen printer's most important tools.

designed for screen printing. Other types of ink will not work correctly. They can even damage your screen.

Some professional screen printers use pure **pigments** to mix their own ink. The process for doing that would fill an entire book on its own. It is unnecessary to mix your own inks from scratch because you can buy screen printing ink in a variety of colors. But sometimes you might want a color that you can't buy premixed. In these situations, you can mix different colored inks together before you print.

Another necessary tool for screen printing is a squeegee. This is a piece of flexible plastic with a wooden handle. It should ideally be the same width as your screen. You will use it to pull ink across the screen, pushing it down onto the surface you are printing on. Like the other tools you need, squeegees can be purchased at most art supply stores.

Once you have gathered all the tools for creating your screen print, you need to choose the material on which you'll be printing. This is often called a **substrate**. Common substrates for screen printing include cloth and paper.

Who can screen print, you might be wondering? Anyone! Read on to get started on your own screen printing masterpieces.

Chapter 2

Creating Your Image

Once you have the tools, the next step is to choose the design you'd like to print. The image can be anything you want. It could be an animal, a word, or a logo. Use your imagination! Simpler images are easier to print for beginners. However, once you get good at it, you'll see that screen printing can achieve quite a lot of detail.

Once you practice enough, you can screen print using complex designs and multiple colors.

Simple Shapes

What does *simple* mean when we're talking about a screen printing **stencil**? It means that the shapes you cut out should be large enough to cut without difficulty. For example, if you want to create a stencil with words, use big, blocky letters. You should also keep in mind the space between the shapes that you are cutting out. The smaller those spaces are, the weaker your stencil will be, because you'll be cutting away more of the paper or plastic. You can experiment with different shapes and patterns to see what will and won't work. Trial and error is a great way to learn!

Remember to be very careful when you are cutting out your stencil. Craft knives are sharp, and you could easily cut yourself. Ask an adult for help if you aren't used to using a craft knife.

How do you turn an image into a print? One way involves a method called burning the screen. This makes your image the only area of your screen that ink can be pushed through. We'll get into that later, though. When you're starting out, using a stencil is a bit easier for getting the hang of screen printing. Stencils cannot produce the amount of detail that burned screens can, but they are simpler to use. They also allow you to use one screen to print many different designs without have to go through the process of removing a burned image.

You can use a knife to trim any extra tape from your stencil.

To make a stencil, start by drawing or printing out your image on a piece of paper. Thick, sturdy paper works best, but almost any kind will work. You can also use a sheet of thin plastic. Just remember that your stencil must be resistant to the moisture of the ink. In other words, it can't be something that will fall apart when it gets wet. You don't want your stencil to be destroyed in the middle of printing! If all you have available is a thin piece of computer paper, you can cover it in clear packing tape so it won't disintegrate while you print. Make sure you cover the entire sheet of paper on both sides if you decide to do this. A stencil covered in packing tape will last for about 20 or 30 prints.

There are a few things to keep in mind when choosing a design to print using a stencil. For example, the design must be simple enough to cut out by hand. Too many details will make this difficult. With practice, you will be able to cut out designs with more detail, but it is best to start with simple shapes. Once

Keep a steady hand as you cut out the shapes on your stencil.

you have drawn or printed your image on the paper or plastic, you can cut the design out with scissors or a craft knife.

Once you've got the hang of printing with stencils, you might want to try burning a screen. This will allow you to include more detail in your prints. It will also create a screen that you can use to print the same image over and over again. Burning a screen is a process by which you can make the screen act as your stencil! You will use a chemical process to block off the parts of the screen that you do not want ink to pass through. To perform this process, you will need the following tools and supplies:

- Screen printing liquid called **emulsion**
- A darkroom-safe light
- A tool called a scoop coater (this should be the same width as your screen)
- A clear sheet of plastic that your artwork will be printed on (this is called a transparency)
- A halogen work light

You should be able to buy these items at an art supply store or hardware store. If you can't find them locally, you may need to order them online. There are many brands of emulsion, but any of them should work.

Once you have all of the materials, bring them into a clean work area along with your screen. Set up your darkroom-safe light and mix up your emulsion in a room with no other light coming in. Emulsion is sensitive to **ultraviolet** (UV) light, which is why you need a darkroom-safe light. This light doesn't give off UV rays like regular lightbulbs and sunlight do, so it lets you see what you're doing when you're mixing your emulsion. If you mix up your emulsion where UV light can reach it, it will start to harden right away.

Mix up your emulsion by following the instructions on the bottle. The steps vary depending on the brand, but the process should be simple. Once your emulsion is mixed up, you're ready to coat the screen. Pour your mixed emulsion into the U-shaped section of your scoop coater. Be sure to hold the coater so no emulsion drips out. Tilt your screen up at an angle. Hold the coater at the very bottom of the screen, tilted so the emulsion is touching the screen. Pull your scoop coater upward across the mesh, coating it with the emulsion.

Now that your screen is coated, it will need to dry for a few days. Leave it facedown in the dark. You can

Emulsion

Be sure to coat your screen with an even layer of emulsion.

put it in a cardboard box or a suitcase to make sure that no light gets in. Allow it to dry for two to five days.

Once the emulsion on your screen is dry, you're ready to transfer your image to the mesh. For this part of the process, you'll need a halogen work light, your artwork printed on a transparency, your darkroom-safe light, and a hose. The idea is that you want as much UV light directed toward your screen as possible. Halogen lamps are good for this.

Start by turning off all lights other than your darkroom-safe light. Lay your screen on a table and place the transparency on top of it. Now position your halogen light so it is facing the screen directly. Turn your darkroom-safe light off and turn the halogen light on. Allow the screen to be exposed to the halogen light for five minutes. The emulsion underneath the clear parts of the transparency will begin to harden.

After your screen is done exposing, turn off your halogen light and turn on your darkroom-safe light. The areas of emulsion that were blocked from the light

Burned screens can show more detail than stenciled designs.

need to be washed from the screen. You can do this with a hose or with a spray attachment on a kitchen sink. Do this at night or with your darkroom-safe light, to make sure that the emulsion you're spraying away isn't exposed to any UV light.

Once you've washed off the excess emulsion, your screen will be ready to print.

After you gently spray your screen, the artwork that you had printed on your transparency should be the only part of the screen that isn't blocked by hardened, exposed emulsion. This means that when you push ink through the screen, only your design will be printed.

Screen printing isn't just for making shirts. You can print designs on totes, posters, and many other objects.

Chapter 3

Final Preparations

Once your stencil or exposed screen is ready, gather up the rest of the materials you'll need. These include your clean, dry screen, a squeegee, a substrate to print on (we'll be using

It's best to get all of your materials together before you start the printing process.

Choose a clean shirt that is large enough to fit your entire design.

Smoothing Out Substrates

It's important that your substrate is very **taut** and flat. If you're using a shirt or some other cloth substrate, you need to make sure there aren't any wrinkles in it, either. A loose or wrinkled substrate often results in an uneven or blurred image. It might also cause the image to print with gaps in it. Some people steam or iron their substrates before printing on them to make sure they are completely free of wrinkles.

T-shirts and sweatshirts), cardboard, ink, and a friend to assist you.

Clear off a flat, steady table to use as your printing area. Put the cardboard inside the shirt. Make sure that your cardboard is large enough to keep the shirt stretched taut. Smooth out any wrinkles on the side

Make sure you don't get your shirt twisted at an odd angle as you put the cardboard inside.

you'll be printing on. Lay the taut shirt on the table, printing side up.

If you're using a stencil, lay it on the shirt wherever you'd like your design to be printed. Since you only want your design to be printed onto the shirt, cover the surrounding area of the shirt with paper or plastic. This will protect it from accidental splotches of ink that might drip as you work.

Lay your screen slowly onto the stencil and shirt. Be sure that it is laying flat and that you didn't shift the stencil or surrounding paper. Have a friend hold the screen in place so it won't shift at all during the printing process. If the screen moves while you're printing, the stencil will likely shift as well. This will cause your printed image to smudge on the shirt.

Use a spoon, a knife, or a tool called a palette knife to lay down a line of ink on the screen about 2 inches (5 centimeters) above where your stenciled image is placed on the shirt. The line should extend 1 or 2 inches (2.5 or 5 cm) past your stencil to ensure that you won't miss the edges of the design when you pull the ink down. This line of ink should be about as wide as a finger. Now get your squeegee ready. It's time to print.

Chapter 4

Time to Print!

Hold the squeegee firmly with both of your hands so you can apply even pressure with it when you pull the ink across the screen. Line the squeegee up above the ink and press it down onto the screen. Your friend should still be holding down the screen firmly against the table as you pull the ink across the mesh.

Steadily pull the squeegee down across your design. Use a lot of downward force to be sure you're pushing the ink through the mesh. Push the ink back up to the top of the screen and pull back down across your

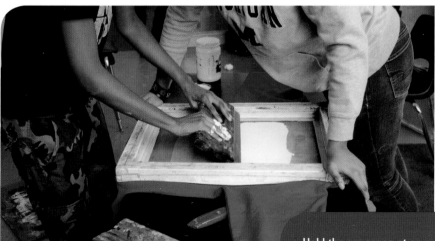

Hold the squeegee at an angle as you pull it across the screen.

stencil about three times. Before you lift up the screen, make sure to flood it with ink. This simply means one last pull without downward pressure, leaving the screen full of ink. If you need to pause during printing for any reason, make sure that the screen is flooded. This will prevent the ink from drying in the screen, which can be difficult to clean later on. It can even make a screen unusable if you're not careful. If you don't flood the screen, the layer of ink that is left in the mesh is so thin that it can dry very quickly. A flooded screen will have enough moisture to prevent that from happening. After flooding the screen, lift it up very slowly to reveal your screen printed shirt.

A Smooth Pull

Pulling ink across a screen with a squeegee will become second nature with practice. Just remember when you're starting out to keep a constant amount of downward pressure as you pull the ink. Try not to pause in the middle of your image. The idea is to evenly coat your substrate with ink so large globs of ink don't linger on any one spot on your screen. These drops and blobs of ink can sneak under your stencil and create errors in your final print.

Congratulations! You've officially made a screen print! If you want to be able to keep printing, you need to take very good care of your tools. You need to clean the screen as soon as possible after removing it from the shirt. Otherwise, the ink will dry on the screen. Run the screen under water, scrubbing it gently with a rag, sponge, or paper towel until it

Cleaning up is an important part of the screen printing process.

is clean. Do the same with your squeegee. Before printing again, make sure that your screen and squeegee are dry. A print won't turn out well if you use a wet screen. You can use a blow-dryer to dry your screen more quickly, if necessary.

Once your tools are clean, go back to your shirt and carefully take the cardboard out so that you can use it for your next print. Lay the shirt over the back of a chair or on a flat surface to dry. Your shirt will be dry and ready to wear in less than an hour. If you want it to dry faster, you can use a blow-dryer on the ink to speed up the process.

Keep It Clean

Though it's not anybody's favorite part of printing, cleanup is one of the most important steps. Screen printing ink typically dries very fast, and it is difficult to remove once it's dry. This makes sense if you think about it. You wouldn't want your dry ink coming off of your shirt when you wash it. You should clean your tools as quickly and as thoroughly as possible after every printing session you complete. This will allow you to continue printing as often as you want to!

Now that you've printed a shirt, what will you make next? A poster of your own original artwork? Invitations to your next birthday party? Custom sweatshirts for all of your friends? Use your imagination and keep trying new things. You never know what incredible projects you might come up with!

Once you're done, you can show off your new creation by wearing it.

Glossary

emulsion (i-MUHL-shuhn) a mixture of two liquids in which the particles of one liquid mix with the other liquid but do not dissolve

makers (MAY-kurz) people who use their creativity to make something

pigments (PIG-muhnts) substances that give color to something; pigments can be natural, as in people's skin, or added to something, as in paint

printmaking (PRINT-may-king) the process of creating printed artwork on paper, cloth, or other surfaces

stencil (STEN-suhl) a piece of paper, plastic, or metal with letters or a pattern cut out of it

substrate (SUHB-strayt) a flat surface on which an artist creates a print

taut (TAWT) stretched tight

ultraviolet (uhl-truh-VYE-uh-lit) a type of light that cannot be seen by the human eye; it is given off by the sun and most other common light sources

warp (WORP) get twisted, curved, or bent out of shape

Find Out More

BOOKS

Grabowski, Beth. *Printmaking: A Complete Guide to Materials & Processes.* Upper Saddle River, N.J. : Prentice Hall, 2009.

Paparone, Nick. *Print Liberation: The Screen Printing Primer.* Cincinnati, OH: F+W Publications, 2008.

WEB SITES

Instructables: DIY Screen Printing
www.instructables.com/id /Screenprinting-Easy-Detailed-Inexpensive/
Check out another method for creating simple screen printed designs.

Index

aluminum, 7

burning a screen, 12, 15–20

cardboard, 23, 28
cleanup, 26, 27–28
craft knives, 12, 15

Detroit Community High (DCH) Apparel, 6
drying, 8, 16–17, 26, 27, 28

emulsion, 15, 16, 18–19
errors, 26

flooding, 26
frames, 7–8

ink, 8–9, 13, 15, 23, 24, 25, 26, 27, 28

nylon, 7

pressure, 25, 26

scoop coaters, 15, 16

squeegees, 9–10, 21, 24, 25, 26, 28
stencils, 12–15, 24, 26
substrates, 10, 21, 22, 23, 26
supplies, 6–10, 15

transparencies, 15, 17, 18

ultraviolet (UV) light, 16, 17–18, 19

wrinkles, 22, 23–24

About the Authors

Lyz Luidens graduated from the University of Michigan Penny Stamps School of Art & Design in 2013. She is a founding member of Detroit's Riopelle artist collective and a co-owner/printer at PranksterPress, a fine art and printmaking studio housed in Riopelle.

Camille Griffin is a senior at Detroit Community High School. She is an A and B student with a passion for art. In her junior year, she joined the Detroit Community High School Entrepreneurship in Action program where she discovered screen printing.

Special thanks to Angel Brown and Justin Williamson for their help with the book.